Weapons of Fantasy and Folklore

by John Hamilton

Visit us at

WWW.ABDOPUB.COM

Published by ABDO Publishing Company, 4940 Viking Drive, Suite 622, Edina, Minnesota 55435.
Copyright ©2006 by Abdo Consulting Group, Inc. International copyrights reserved in all countries.
No part of this book may be reproduced in any form without written permission from the publisher.
ABDO & Daughters™ is a trademark and logo of ABDO Publishing Company.

Printed in the United States.

Editor: Paul Joseph
Graphic Design: John Hamilton
Cover Design: TDI
Cover Illustration: *Kai Feng* ©1989 Don Maitz
Interior Photos and Illustrations: p 1 *Curse of Sagamore* ©1985 Don Maitz;
p 4 parts of a sword, Corbis;
p 5 *Kai Feng* ©1989 Don Maitz; p 6 reenactor with broadsword, Corbis; p 7 *Peril's Gate*, ©2000 Janny
Wurts; p 8 (top) scimitar, Corbis; p 8 (middle) falchion; p 8 (bottom) katana and wakizashi, Getty
Images; p 9 *Knight Corporal*, ©1996 Don Maitz; p 10 Frodo wields Sting, courtesy New Line Cinema;
p 11 King Arthur receives Excalibur, Corbis; p 12 dagger, Getty Images; p 13 *Grand Conspiracy* ©1998
Janny Wurts; p 14 (left) warrior with mace, Mary Evans Picture Library; p 14 (right) war hammer,
courtesy Ritter Steele and Knights Edge; p 15 (top) *Lion of Ireland*, ©1980 Don Maitz; p 15 (bottom)
Sebastion struck by flail, Mary Evans Picture Library; p 16 (left) warrior with spear, Arthur Rackham;
p 16 (right) spear head, Corbis; p 17 (top) halberds, ©2005 John Hamilton; p 17 (bottom) knights in
battle, Corbis; p 18 Battle of Crécy, Corbis; p 19 *Archer* ©1996 Don Maitz; p 20 *Bard IV*, ©1987 Don
Maitz; p 21 (top) reloading crossbow, Corbis; p 21 (bottom) soldiers with longbow and crossbow, Mary
Evans Picture Library; p 22 *Swordsman*, ©1996 Don Maitz; p 23 *Knight Captain*, ©1996 Don Maitz; p
24 Lancelot and Tarquine, Mary Evans Picture Library; p 25 (top) great helm, ©2005 John Hamilton;
p 25 (bottom) armored foot in stirrup, ©2005 John Hamilton; p 26 armor of Henry VIII, ©2005 John
Hamilton; p 27 plate armor, ©2005 John Hamilton; p 28 (top) German Shepherd, Corbis; p 28 (bottom)
elephants in battle, Mary Evans Picture Library; p 29 (top) fell beast, courtesy New Line Cinema; p 29
(bottom) oliphaunts, courtesy New Line Cinema; p 31, warriors ready for battle, courtesy New Line
Cinema.

Library of Congress Cataloging-in-Publication Data

Hamilton, John, 1959–
    Weapons of fantasy and folklore / John Hamilton
        p. cm. — (Fantasy & folklore)
    Includes index.
    ISBN 1-59679-340-6
    1. Weapons—Mythology—Juvenile literature. 2. Weapons—Folklore—Juvenile literature.
3. Fantasy literature—History and criticism—Juvenile literature.   I. Title

    U800.H345 2006
    623.4—dc22
                                                                2005048277

CONTENTS

SWORDS

 sword is perhaps the best-known weapon of any knight's arsenal. It was an essential piece of equipment, as important to a knight as his horse and armor. Many knights named their swords. Some swords were highly prized, passed down as heirlooms from generation to generation.

Swords were high-tech pieces of equipment for the Middle Ages. Making them required specialized knowledge of metallurgy. Carbonized iron was turned to steel, which was hammered to finely-crafted blades with razor-sharp edges. Swords were so deadly that in the trained hands of a knight, they could easily lop off limbs, or cut a foe in two. A prized sword could be an expensive weapon, affordable only by the richest knights.

Swords were made in a large variety of shapes and sizes. Some were short and light. Some were huge, used only by the strongest warriors. However, most swords weighed less than three pounds (1.4 kg), and were used with one hand. A popular variation was called a "hand-and-a-half" sword. Its grip was big enough so that it could be wielded with either one hand or two.

Right: The parts of a sword.
Facing page: Kai Feng, by fantasy artist Don Maitz.

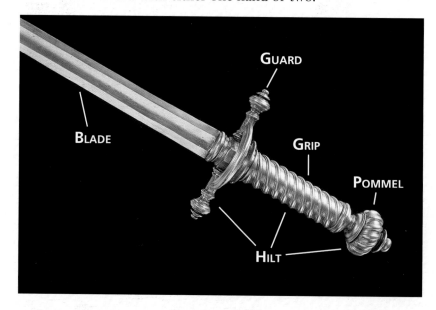

GUARD

BLADE

GRIP

POMMEL

HILT

A medieval sword had four main parts: blade, cross-guard, hilt (or grip), and pommel. Blades were usually straight and double-edged, which meant they were sharpened on both sides. At the beginning of the Middle Ages, sword blades were wide and slightly rounded at the tip. These *broadswords* were used for chopping and slashing attacks, similar to an axe.

A sword's pommel was very important. A pommel was a knob-like feature at the top of the sword's grip. It was designed as a counterweight to the blade. A finely designed pommel made a sword well-balanced, and easier to handle.

After the 1350s, many swords became narrower, stiffer, and had a sharper point. These *longswords* were used because knights were wearing tougher armor. Metal plate armor had become popular during this time. Older sword techniques didn't work as well. Plate armor absorbed the blows of a broadsword's edge. But a powerful thrust with a pointed longsword might find a gap in even the best-made plate armor.

Sword design continually changed to meet the needs of medieval combat. Late in the Middle Ages, during the 15th century, armor became too expensive for many soldiers. Sword blades again were made thicker, as slashing attacks were used once more on the battlefield. By this time, shields weren't as commonly used, thanks to the protection of plate armor. Instead of using a shield to block a foe's swing, knights learned how to block sword thrusts with their own sword, which was called parrying. Sometimes a fighter might parry a blow, get in close to his opponent, and then strike him in the face or head with the pommel of his sword. This is where we get the phrase "to pommel," or "to pummel" someone.

Left: A reenactor dressed in mail armor wields a broadsword.
Facing page: Peril's Gate, by Janny Wurts.

There were many other commonly used swords in the Middle Ages. *Shortswords* were very popular. They were double-edged, with a blade usually less than two feet (.6 m) in length.

A true *two-handed sword*, unlike a "hand-and-a-half" sword, was huge, upwards of six feet (1.8 m) in length. It took special training to use these heavy swords.

A *scimitar* was a curved-bladed single-edged sword, specially suited for slashing attacks. They were especially popular in the Middle East. A *saber* is a kind of scimitar, used for troops attacking on horseback.

A *falchion* was a short sword with a curved, single-edged blade. The non-cutting edge was squared off so that it looked like a big kitchen knife. Falchions were popular weapons used mainly by foot soldiers.

In medieval Japan, famed warriors called samurai carried two swords, both with curved, single-edged blades. The quality of samurai swords is legendary. The longer weapon was called a *katana*. It had a hilt covered with braided fabric so the samurai's fingers wouldn't slip in combat. The shorter sword was called a *wakizashi*. Like the katana, it was used in combat, and also in a form of ritual suicide called *seppuku*.

Above (top): A scimitar.
Above: A falchion used in battle.
Right: A martial artist wields a katana in his right hand, and the shorter wakizashi blade in his left.
Facing page: A soldier wields a shortsword in *Knight Corporal,* by Don Maitz.

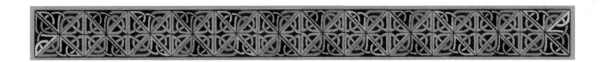

In many legends and stories of fantasy, swords had an almost magical quality, as if they were living characters. Probably the most famous legendary sword was Excalibur, the sword of Arthur, king of the Britons.

Legend says that Excalibur was a gift from the Lady of the Lake, who was an enchantress second in power only to Merlin the magician. Excalibur's blade was unbreakable. It could slice through steel or stone without losing its razor-sharp edge. In battle, it shone like a torch. When wielding Excalibur, together with its jewel-encrusted scabbard, King Arthur could never be defeated, or even wounded, in battle.

Excalibur was not the same sword as the famous sword in the stone, the blade that Arthur drew from sold rock to signify that he alone had the right to be king. Arthur broke that sword in a duel with King Pellinore. Arthur's cause in that fight was unjust, and violated his right to be king. After the sword was broken, Arthur realized the mistake he'd made, and was sorry for the harm he'd done. To replace the sword, Merlin took Arthur to a secret lake deep in the woods. Emerging from the surface of the water was a pale arm that held a magnificent sword, Excalibur. The Lady of the Lake then gave the sword to a grateful Arthur.

Facing page: King Arthur, accompanied by Merlin, is given the sword Excalibur and its magic scabbard by the Lady of the Lake. *Below:* Frodo Baggins wields the sword Sting in the lair of Shelob, the giant spider, in *The Return of the King.*

There are several magical swords in the fantasy world of J.R.R. Tolkien's *The Lord of the Rings*. The sword Narsil was wielded by the high-king Elendil, and later by his son Isildur, in the battle at Barad-dûr against the evil Sauron. Narsil was a legendary blade that "shone with the light of the sun and of the moon." During the fight, Sauron shattered the sword into shards, before he himself was defeated by Isildur. Many years later, the shards were reforged into a new sword called Andúril, which was used by the hero Aragorn in *The Return of the King.*

Even the tiny Bilbo Baggins, in his adventures in *The Hobbit*, had a magical sword. Called Sting, it was a shortsword, just the right size for a small hobbit. Sting glowed blue light in the presence of enemies, especially orcs. Bilbo eventually gave Sting to his nephew Frodo before the younger hobbit embarked on his own quest in *The Lord of the Rings.*

DAGGERS

 aggers were usually double-edged. Sometimes they had a single edge, like an oversized table knife. They could be held in one hand and used for slashing or stabbing. Knights and other men-at-arms often carried a dagger as a secondary weapon, just in case their main weapon became lost or damaged.

Daggers came in many different shapes and sizes. Some looked like miniature swords, while others were specially shaped depending on how they were used. Some had straight blades, others curved or tapered. Some were short, while others were as long as 20 inches (51 cm), which was almost as long as a short-sword. Early daggers, from about A.D. 1000 to 1150, were shaped more like big kitchen knives. This kind of early knife was called a *cultellus*, which is where we get the modern word *cutlass*.

Some daggers had special purposes on the battlefield. In India, a *peshkabz* dagger had a very sharp point and a strong spine so that is could be thrust through mail armor. In France, the *misericorde* dagger was built long and narrow. When a knight got knocked to the ground, a soldier using a misericorde thrust the dagger through openings in the unfortunate warrior's armor.

During the Hundred Years' War between England and France in the 14th and 15th centuries, there are many stories of knights using their daggers as missiles. As two groups of knights marched toward each other in battle, they threw their daggers (along with their axes and maces) at each other before getting close enough for sword combat.

Right: A dagger with an ornate hilt. *Facing page:* This hero wields both a sword and a dagger in *Grand Conspiracy*, by Janny Wurts.

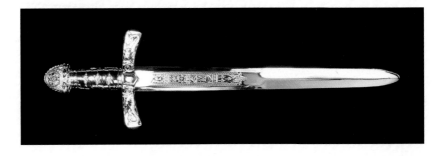

Axes and Maces

arriors have used axes, in one form or another, for thousands of years. Stone-Age people used wooden handles with sharpened blocks of flint as axe heads. Primitive and barbarian warrior cultures liked axes because they could be used both as weapons and tools. By the Middle Ages, axes had evolved into wicked steel-headed weapons that could slice through limbs or chop off unprotected heads.

Many knights preferred a good, sturdy axe rather than a sword. Some even fought on horseback with a long-handled version. A *bardiche* was an extra-strong kind of axe. It took two hands to swing. It was so sturdy and sharp that it could sometimes hack through a knight's plate armor.

Early clubs were simple weapons, made of a single piece of wood. During medieval times, composite clubs were made that had a wood or metal handle, with a head made of stone or metal. A *war hammer* was similar in shape to an axe, except the head was a stout metal pick designed for crushing armor or bone.

A *mace* was like a metal club with protruding flanges on the head. It was designed not only to dent and break an opponent's armor, but even to pierce it. Some maces, called *morning stars*,

Lower right: A war hammer.
Below: A medieval warrior armed with a mace.

had spiky pieces of metal protruding from the head for just this purpose. Of course, a blow from a morning star on unprotected flesh would be devastating as well.

The name morning star is often wrongly given to a metal ball attached by a short chain to a wooden or metal handle.

These weapons are more correctly called *military flails*. Sometimes the ball had sharp metal spikes protruding from it. An armored knight could quickly devastate groups of unprotected foot soldiers by whirling the flail and dashing into the melee.

Above: Lion of Ireland, by Don Maitz.
Left: Sebastian, the king of Portugal, is about to be struck dead by a mounted warrior armed with a military flail, during an ill-fated invasion of Morocco in 1578.

15

SPEARS AND LANCES

Spears are one of the world's oldest weapons. Stone-Age people hunted wild game more than 20,000 years ago using sharp pieces of flint tied to long sticks. As civilization developed, so too did the design of these ancient weapons. There were many kinds of spears used in warfare. Spear tips could be simple steel points, or have long, elaborate bladed edges like a sword. Some spears were short, others measured more than 18 feet (5.5 m) long, such as the *pike*, a thrusting spear first developed by the ancient Greeks about 300 B.C.

Ancient Romans invented a clever type of throwing spear called a *pilum*. It had a small, leaf-shaped blade on the end of a long iron neck, which was mounted on a wooden shaft. If a Roman soldier, called a legionnaire, hurled the pilum and it stuck in a foe's shield, the slender shaft bent downward. The weight of the spear made the shield heavy and unbalanced. Even if the enemy managed

Left: Archaeologists estimate that this spearhead is more than 2,600 years old. *Far left:* A warrior carries a spear in this painting by Arthur Rackham.

to pry the pilum free, he couldn't hurl it back at the legionnaire because it was damaged. Medieval Franks and Anglo-Saxons had a similar type of throwing spear called an *angon*.

Halberds and glaives had long, sharp blades with pointed tips like a spear, with the addition of projecting spikes on the back of the blade. They were used like an axe on a very long wooden pole, about 6 to 8 feet (1.8 to 2.4 m) long. Halberds and glaives were very deadly, and were especially good at attacking and pulling down knights mounted on horseback.

Besides a sword, a medieval knight's most trusted weapon was his lance. A lance was a long, tapering wooden spear about 9 to 11 feet (2.7 to 3.4 m) in length, with a small metal tip that was sometimes bladed. A knight on horseback used his lance by tucking the butt-end under the arm and then charging at his foe. When two knights attacked each other, the impact was tremendous. A lance attack was especially devastating because the weight of the horse was added to the force of the blow. Even hardened plate armor could be pierced by a skillfully used lance.

Above: Halberds on display at the Tower of London.
Below: A page from a medieval manuscript showing knights in battle using swords and lances.

bows

 ne of the most feared weapons on the medieval battlefield was the longbow. Starting in the 14th century, it was the chief weapon of English armies, until firearms became more common in the 16th and 17th centuries. Before this time period, shorter bows were used for defense and for hunting, but it was difficult to attack knights because of the armor they wore.

The longbow, obviously, was much longer than a common short bow. Nearly as long as a man was tall, longbows usually measured five to six feet (1.5 to 1.8 m), with arrows at least a yard (.9 m) long. The longbow was tremendously powerful. It had a range of about 230 to 250 yards (210 to 229 m), about two and a half times the length of a football field. Arrows shot from a longbow could easily penetrate mail armor.

Although it is commonly called an "English longbow," its origin is actually Wales. Eventually, English kings trained their own fighters to use longbows. Unlike the Welsh, who used the weapon in small-group sneak attacks, the English used groups of up to 500 archers, all shooting at once, at a rate of 12 shots per minute. The results of such a fearsome attack could be devastating.

In 1346, near the village of Crécy, in northern France, 6,000 English archers virtually destroyed an entire French army of knights and men-at-arms. On that stormy summer evening, helped

Facing page: Archer, by Don Maitz. *Below:* English longbowmen win the day at the Battle of Crécy in 1346.

by several hundred English knights, the archers unleashed wave after wave of deadly arrows. After 90 minutes of fighting, 5,542 French knights lay dead on the battlefield. Armies could no longer ignore the power of the longbow.

Longbows were not perfect weapons. Their weakness was that it took tremendous strength to fire them, and the archer had to be well-practiced to hit the target. *Crossbows* had an advantage over traditional bows because they used stored-up mechanical power instead of muscles. It didn't take as much practice to learn to fire a crossbow. Also, crossbows could be kept cocked and ready to fire for much longer than bows. Unfortunately, it took a long time to reload a crossbow. A skilled longbowman could fire 12 arrows in the same time it took a

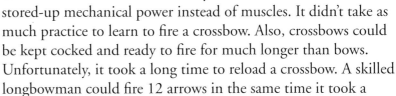

soldier armed with a crossbow to reload and fire his weapon.

The first crossbows were used in Europe in the 11th century. Over the next few centuries, crossbow technology developed to make them more and more powerful, and easier to reload. Crossbows fired metal bolts about half the size of an arrow. They were fired with such force that crossbow bolts could penetrate most armor worn by knights. Crossbows were so deadly that the Church tried to ban them, but the order was mostly ignored.

Facing page: Bard IV, by Don Maitz. *Right:* A soldier reloads his crossbow using a hand crank. *Below:* Soldiers carrying a longbow and a crossbow.

ARMOR

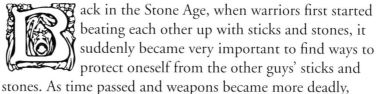

Back in the Stone Age, when warriors first started beating each other up with sticks and stones, it suddenly became very important to find ways to protect oneself from the other guys' sticks and stones. As time passed and weapons became more deadly, personal armor also evolved to meet this growing threat.

The challenge in making effective armor is to build it strong enough to repel any attack, yet light enough so a warrior can still do his job on the battlefield. Although most fantasy stories focus on armor created in medieval Europe and the Middle East, armor was developed by almost every culture on Earth. Some armor was very advanced. Countries often adopted armor styles from other competing nations and improved on them. For example, Chinese-style armor was borrowed by Japan and altered to form the elegant armor worn by Japan's fearsome samurai warriors.

Very early armor was primitive, but somewhat effective against the weapons of the time. A tunic, or long coat, of hard leather was often all that stood between a warrior's flesh and a whirling metal blade.

Left: In *Swordsman,* a painting by Don Maitz, a warrior is dressed mainly in hard leather armor.
Facing page: Knight Captain, by Don Maitz. This man is dressed in fanciful plate armor.

Starting around the 5th and 6th centuries, armor makers created garments made from small iron rings interlocked together. This kind of armor was called *mail.* Today it is often referred to as "chain-mail," but most medieval people simply called it mail. Shirts of mail were called *hauberks* in Europe, except by the Norse people of Scandinavia, including the Vikings, who called their armor *byrnies.* A full hauberk or byrnie weighed about 30 pounds (13.6 kg).

Eventually, knights began to clad their entire bodies in mail armor, not only shirts but also hoods, leggings, and gloves. It took a long time to make a garment of mail. Each link was interlocked with four neighboring links. Over 30,000 iron links were needed just to make one mail shirt.

Mail was a flexible fabric, and very hard. It could protect a knight from most cutting blows, such as from a sword. It wasn't very good, however, at stopping the piercing attacks of spears or arrows. The narrow points of arrows shot by English longbows sailed right through the rings of mail.

To help protect against such attacks, warriors also carried shields into battle. (Of course, shields gave protection against

Below: Sir Lancelot, in blue, and Sir Tarquine, each dressed in mail armor, face off against each other. Each knight wields a broadsword and kite-shaped shield. Painting by N.C. Wyeth.

sword and axe attacks as well.) Shields came in many shapes and sizes during the Middle Ages. Footmen, including Norse warriors such as the Vikings, preferred round-shaped shields. Knights used shields that were kite-shaped. Some had a notch cut into the right-hand corner to support a couched lance.

Most shields in medieval Europe were made of layers of thick wooden boards glued together, much like today's plywood. The wood was covered with a hard material like leather or plaster. The outside of many shields were colorfully decorated, usually with the knight's coat of arms.

As weapons became more deadly, better armor than mail was needed to protect knights, especially armor that could stop piercing attacks. Around the middle of the 14th century, armor made from steel or hard-iron plates became very popular. This was the beginning of the age of knights in shining armor, the image most of us have of knights and chivalry.

Plate armor was cut into various sizes and then hammered into shapes to fit different parts of the body. Each knight had his plate armor custom fitted. Precise measurements were needed to ensure a proper fit. Otherwise, a knight wouldn't be able to move around very well on the battlefield.

A knight's full collection of plate armor was not called a "suit of armor." In medieval times, it was simply called "an armor," or a "harness." "Suit of armor" is a relatively modern expression that wasn't used until about 1600, well after the age of knights and chivalry.

Above: A great helm had a narrow slit through which the knight could see. It got very hot inside the helm, but it gave the knight some protection from cutting blows against the head.
Left: A foot wrapped in plate armor, resting in a metal stirrup.

Above: Plate armor worn by English King Henry VIII and his horse.

The most important parts of a harness of armor included a *great helm* to protect the entire head, a *neckguard*, a *breastplate* for the chest, *gauntlets* for the hands and forearms, and *greaves* to cover the feet and lower legs. Straps and buckles, and sometimes spring catches, were used to fasten the pieces together.

Plate armor took a long time to make, and was very expensive. Toward the end of the Middle Ages, it became so elaborate and so specialized to make that only rich nobles could afford a full harness of plate armor. It might cost a knight the same amount of money as we would pay today for a small house or expensive sports car. For knights who couldn't afford a full set of armor, they made do with a cheaper-quality helm and breastplate. Some couldn't even afford this minimal protection.

Today we often think of lumbering knights unable to move around, encased in their armor, so heavy that cranes and winches were needed to hoist them into their horse's saddles. This is a myth that comes mainly from Mark Twain's book, *A Connecticut Yankee in King Arthur's Court*. In fact, a full harness of plate armor was relatively light, weighing less than 60 pounds (27 kg). This is lighter than the gear carried by most of today's soldiers. Also, knights in armor were very nimble. Many could leap onto their horse without even touching their feet to the stirrups!

Remember, a knight's armor was specially fitted to his body, and he had been training since childhood to fight.

Plate armor was hard, like glass, but not brittle. You could barely scratch it. During the later medieval period, good plate armor was so smooth, hard, and polished that almost any weapon would glance off harmlessly. Even an arrow shot from the feared English longbow usually bounced off the toughest plate armor.

Plate armor did have its weaknesses. Occasionally, a tremendous blow from an axe or war hammer was enough to break through. Even if a blow didn't pierce the armor, it was often enough to give the knight a concussion, break his bones, or damage his internal organs. Also, wearing a full harness of plate armor was very hot and stuffy. At the Battle of Agincourt in 1415, in northern France, England's Duke of York (King Henry V's uncle) died from heatstroke in his armor.

By the 15th century, handguns began changing the face of war. Lead bullets, propelled by explosive charges of gunpowder, punched through even the toughest plate armor. For many decades afterwards, proud and stubborn knights continued using armor for protection. But by the second quarter of the 16th century, as handguns and cannons became more and more powerful and cheaper to manufacture, it became clear that the age of knights and chivalry was quickly drawing to a close.

Below: Plate armor on exhibit at England's Tower of London, showing a great helm, neckguard, breastplate, and gauntlets.

EASTS

People have been fighting animals since they first learned how to hunt. It should come as no surprise to learn that armies have used beasts as weapons of war. Today, the thought of using innocent animals to kill is repelling to most people. But in the Middle Ages, it happened quite often. Back then, it was cruel, but not unusual.

Knights, of course, rode horses. However, a huge warhorse could do more than simply transport warriors into battle. Medieval warhorses were trained to tolerate the smell of blood. They sometimes had their hooves sharpened,

Right: A German Shepherd military attack dog.
Below: Elephants attack the army of Alexander the Great.

and would trample an enemy soldier at the knight's command. Warhorses were often fitted with special armor, either mail or plate.

Dogs, especially large breeds like mastiffs, have long been used in warfare. Some wardogs were fitted with armor and spiked collars. It was common to unleash groups of dogs in order to break up lines of enemy troops. Some knights kept a wardog in the saddle with them, unleashing them at the right moment to tear apart some poor footman.

Elephants, huge and deadly, were used by many armies on the battlefield. Alexander the Great first saw them used during his military campaign in India. He was so impressed that in 325 B.C. he began using them in his own army. Not only could elephants trample the enemy, they could also carry troops into battle,

much like modern armored troop carriers. Some elephants even carried oversized swords in their trunks. This sight must have been frightening indeed to any foot soldier unfortunate enough to be caught in the rampaging pachyderm's path.

In the world of fantasy, beasts are used regularly on the battlefield. Dragons make many appearances, perhaps most famously in Anne McCaffrey's *Dragonriders of Pern* series of books. In J.R.R. Tolkien's *The Return of the King*, enormous, elephant-like creatures called *oliphaunts* wreaked havoc during the Battle of the Pelennor Fields in front of the city of Minas Tirith.

Also in *The Return of the King*, evil servants of the villain Sauron, called the Nazgûl, rode on great winged pterosaur-like creatures called *fell beasts*.

Above: The hobbit Frodo Baggins confronts a Nazgûl riding a fell beast, in *The Return of the King.*
Below: Oliphaunts at the Battle of the Pelennor Fields.

GLOSSARY

ANGLO-SAXONS

The Germanic people who dominated England from the time of their arrival in the 5th century until the Norman Conquest of 1066. Today it also refers to anyone of English descent.

BARBARIAN

A term used in the Middle Ages for anyone who didn't belong to one of the "great" civilizations such as the Greeks or Romans, or from the Christian kingdoms such as France or Britain.

CHIVALRY

A code of conduct, a kind of way that a knight lived his life. Chivalry demanded bravery, courtesy, generosity, a willingness to help the weak, and most importantly, an undying loyalty to king and country.

COAT OF ARMS

A unique design (right) that distinguishes a person, family, or country. In medieval times, knights painted a coat of arms onto their shields or outer garments in order to be identified in battle.

FOLKLORE

The unwritten traditions, legends, and customs of a culture. Folklore is usually passed down by word of mouth from generation to generation.

MEDIEVAL

Something from the Middle Ages.

MELEE

When two groups of knights at a tournament massed together and fought in hand-to-hand combat. Also a term for any large group of warriors fighting up close on the battlefield.

Armed soldiers line up for battle in Peter Jackson's *The Return of the King.*

MIDDLE AGES

In European history, a period defined by historians as roughly between 476 A.D. and 1450 A.D.

NOBLE

Someone born into a class of people who have high social or political status. Sometimes ordinary people could be made nobles by doing something extraordinary, like fighting well on the battlefield. Usually, however, only people who are the sons or daughters of nobles got to be nobles themselves.

NORSE

The people, language, or culture of Scandinavia, especially medieval Scandinavia. The Vikings were famous Nordic people.

QUEST

A long, difficult search for something important. When the knights of Camelot were searching for the Holy Grail, they were said to be on a quest.

INDEX